It Wasn't
Like This
Before

ALZHEIMER'S

CHARLES BUZZELL

PAGE PUBLISHING, INC.
New York, NY

First originally published by Page Publishing, Inc. 2019

ISBN 978-1-64424-465-4 (Paperback)
ISBN 978-1-64424-466-1 (Digital)

Printed in the United States of America

Contents

It Wasn't Like This Before

With total confusion,
And tears in her eyes,
She said, "It wasn't like
this before."

Now, I do for her, the things,
She once did on her own,
Yes, I know it's not like
it once was anymore.
No, it wasn't like this before.

Over 50 years of marriage,
She's the Mother of our boys,
We've shared, life's ups
and downs together,
Both the heartaches and the joys.

I gladly, help her with the struggle,
She faces every day,
Knowing she would do
the same for me,
If my life turned to gray.

She doesn't understand the change,
Why her days, aren't like before,
It's just not like it once was anymore,
No, it wasn't like this before.

But, as the Good Lord promised,
In the next life He'll restore,
Once again, we'll be together,
Just like it was before.

May 2017 and November 2017

She No Longer Knows My Name

She no longer knows my name,
I'm just an image from the past,
Though our never-ending love,
Will forever last.

Someday we'll stroll together,
In a dwelling, where angels abound,
Once again, she'll know my name,
And her memory will be sound.

Thanks to our Heavenly Father,
With a touch of His healing hand,
He will bring back life eternal,
In His glorious Promised Land.

We will gather with our loved ones,
Who earlier paved the way,
Rejoicing in their comfort,
Patiently waiting…on those
We'll greet someday.

December 2017

Restitution

Thank you for the challenge Lord,
You cast upon our door,
I'll trust that I've been chosen,
To carry out Your plan,
But, I am weak and Thou art strong,
So I'll need a helping hand.

I promise I will pass your test,
Though, I've often failed before,
You've given me a special chance,
To serve the one, whom I adore.

Please swarm our home with angels,
Like bees from a summer hive,
And when helpful sources slumber,
My vowed effort will survive.

She has more than earned repayment,
You have called me to provide,
Though, I'll always be indebted,
To the loved one by my side.

The day the storm clouds gather,
And headwinds cross the land,
She'll be holding hands with Jesus,
I'll have carried out Your plan.

December 2017

Come Here, I Love You

I'm rejoicing for the one I love,
Though, my broken heart opines,
Her soul belongs to Jesus,
Her cherished memory is still mine.

This moment, I'll always treasure,
When she reached with weakened arms,
And clearly said, "Come here, I love you,"
With a smile and her precious charm.

Her captivating beauty,
Was no stranger to my eye,
The warmth, and satin complexion,
Like soft wings of a butterfly.

I know the strength she gathered,
Came from the Lord above,
An unexpected gift to me,
From the one I truly love.

I'm filled with many others,
I replay all the time.
Stored, in the fortress of my heart,
Safe, in the stronghold of my mind.
Yes, the memories are still mine.

A loving husband

Are You Still My Girl?

"Are you still my girl?"
I would often ask,
More than once a day,
And survey her expression,
And wait to hear her say,

"Ah huh, I wah, wah wuv you."

Her words came with a struggle,
But their meaning was still there,
The eloquence was missing,
My thankful heart was unaware.

To share that special moment,
Now means the world to me,
Held captive in my heart forever,
And will never be set free.

When we meet someday in heaven,
I'll ask, more than once a day,
"Are you still my girl?"
And, she'll respond more clearly,
And I know what she will say.

2018

The Last Dance

While holding hands together,
We danced our way to bedtime,
Shuffling down the lighted hall,
As if it was the first time.

Now, far from what it once was,
Her steps were gaged and slow,
Ravaged with an illness,
The failing cause, she did not know.

But her brave and valiant heart,
Overcame a weakened mind,
Her endeavor, always cheerful,
And most memories left behind.

I'm sure that she imagined,
She was dancing like before,
Not knowing in the future,
She'd regain her step once more.

Then, our routine was interrupted,
Now, I weep on bended knees,
She left this world in glory,
And saved the last dance for me.

2018

I Wasn't There to Say Goodbye

You couldn't tell me you were leaving,
I should have known time was nigh,
I chose to come back later,
I wasn't there to say goodbye.

My late return, I found you peaceful,
Your precious soul had traveled high,
This new absence left me grieving,
I wasn't there to say goodbye.

Regretful choices have no overs,
When good intentions go awry,
I'm living life with my decision,
I wasn't there to say goodbye.

With our hearts so close together,
It's strange, they failed to amplify,
My blame's in search of reasons,
I wasn't there to say goodbye.

Could I have heard "Come here, I love you,"
One last time?
Those may have been your parting words,
Had your heart consulted mine.

Then Jesus said, "It's not goodbye forever,"
Maybe that's the reason why,
When again we meet each other,
It's a big hello and not goodbye.

April 15, 2018

Adrianne's Transition

She'll be waiting for the loved ones,
She sadly leaves behind,
While embracing her dear mother,
She's been missing for some time.

Then, two brothers and a sister,
With stride, step up in line,
And greet their precious sister,
Whose turn it was this time.

Not missing is her father,
Who left them long ago,
Rejoicing with his daughter,
Her warmth he misses so.

Here come the aunts and uncles,
Grandmas, grandpas, cousins too.
The joyous jubilee continues,
Assembled friends and family on review.

This celestial celebration,
Will expand through endless time,
And someday,
She'll greet each loved one,
She once sadly left behind.

I promised I will join her,
In the meantime, I will pray,
The good Lord keeps my pledge in mind,
I look forward to that day.

2018

Had I Been the First to Go

Her life with special meaning,
Defined my path, and made me grow,
A privilege I'd be missing
Had I been the first to go.

Her love was my possession,
Her needs I learned to know,
A chance I may have failed to meet
Had I been the first to go.

Had I been the first to go,
I wouldn't have this pain today,
But, the pain my heart traded for
Took my loved one's pain away.

The gift that her life taught me,
Was the plan for me to stay,
To prepare her for her journey
And, help ease her on the way.

Had I been the first to go,
Leaving her the price to pay,
She would've welcomed His intended plan
And served until my final day.

May 2, 2018

An Easter Birthday

This year she shares her birthday,
On the day our Savior rose,
She'll be celebrating with Him,
No greater gift could be composed.

She's reminded why He came here,
And the gift to all He gave,
An endless life in heaven,
A redeeming gift for her He saved.

So her first eternal birthday,
With His hand is now engraved,
It won't always fall on Easter,
But will be acclaimed and praised.

Now worldly days behind her,
And angels all around,
They adorn her on this special day,
With a golden birthday crown.

Unlike the crown that Jesus wore,
While hanging from the cross,
She's mindful now to give Him thanks,
For His sacrifice and loss.

2018

An Easter Card

Today, I found an Easter card,
One you gave me, over forty years ago,
You signed it, LOVE FOREVER,
It read, our love would only grow.

I sense, you gave direction,
To your card from days gone by,
To remind, your love's forever,
Now I know the reason why.

At all times, you're a gift from God,
Never taking, always giving,
Recalling your unselfish love,
Helps me, through the pain I'm living.

To night when I find dreamland,
Again, my thoughts will be of you,
No different than the nights before,
Hoping you'll come into view.

Because I have a card,
Signed, LOVE FOREVER,
An Easter Birthday gift for you.

March 28, 2018

Alzheimer's Still Waiting

I prayed, she would be the first survivor,
Perhaps a miracle on the way,
My appeal, and prayers went unrequited,
Then, watched decay from day to day.

I think of lives that could've been,
And those left helpless to endure,
A disease that shortens life,
Without hope, without a cure.

Alzheimer's rages unabated,
The illness offers no reprieve,
Many loved ones lost while waiting
praying science would achieve.

My loved one, was among the many,
I may not live to see the day,
For a first survivor revelation,
Like before, I'm waiting helpless,
Like before, I'll hope and pray.

Meanwhile the good news,
For those who waited, and science failed,
There's no waiting time in Heaven,
Restoration guaranteed,
Eternal life, no disappointments,
When our Saviour takes the lead.

September 3, 2018 (Labor Day)

My Valentine Forever

My sweet valentine is missing,
She won't be here this year,
She'll be occupied with angels,
In her new, celestial sphere.

I can visualize her dancing,
In her smooth, majestic way,
And the thought of me without her,
Leaves me saddened with dismay.

We once danced together often,
She could glide across the floor,
As if propelled with angel wings,
And was about to soar.

With her attractive beauty,
And her captivating smile,
I was proud to be her partner,
And share her gracious style.

But this day I'll be without her,
Still we're bound, her heart and mine,
Again, someday we'll dance together,
She'll forever be my valentine.

February 2018

Waiting

Patiently waiting to hear
from my true love,
Who left two weeks ago,
She failed to say her last goodbye,
Though, it wasn't intended I know.

She was carried away by angels,
On a pillow of satin and lace,
Not doubting her destination,
To a well-earned, heavenly place.

Behold her grand reception,
With Mother, family, and friends,
All gathered in beautiful rapture,
To a welcome that has no end.

I'm sure she'll make a visit,
It's only a matter of time,
Someday, when least expected,
She'll soothe this heart of mine.

February 2, 2018

A Picture That I Planned

A picture that I planned, with the one
I started loving over fifty years ago.
How we came together, I remember,
And how our love began to grow.

We both knew, right from the start,
When our craving hearts, became entwined,
Binding hope and dreams together,
Both her precious heart and mine.

We together faced life's struggles,
And lived, one chapter at a time,
Portrayed with love, that's all we knew,
And found no peaks we couldn't climb.

Then the picture book I planned,
Began to slowly fall apart,
My love's comfort needs changed gravely,
A new chapter, with no restart.

It's not the picture I expected,
Nor the chapter I foresaw,
The picture that I hoped for,
I found had a fatal flaw.

For a month ago today,
We placed
her body in the ground.
Her soul now resting, by our Saviour's hand,
My disappointed heart is aching,

This is not the picture that I planned.

February 25, 2018

When We Meet Again

Someday, I'll wrap my arms around you,
And hold you close again once more,
Meanwhile patiently waiting,
For what our Savior has in store.

I'm trusting He will join us,
I'll do everything I can,
To make sure, we're back together,
And, again, together is His plan.

When I go to bed each night,
I say our usual prayer,
It still ends with "Jesus loves you,"
And I imagine you are there.

When I ask if that was good,
I pretend that you respond,
Like you did when you were here,
Your voice, now echoes from beyond.

I'm trying hard to overcome your loss,
Some days, I don't know where to start,
Then my mind begins to wander,
Your loss is branded on my heart.

I miss so many things about you,
Most, your smile that's so contagious,
So please wait for me in heaven,
When together, we both smile in front of Jesus.

February 26, 2018

Return to Sender

Another day without you,
Another day alone,
This place is just a shelter,
With you gone, it's not a home.

I'm sending this love letter,
Just to let you know,
The loss of you is painful,
So my heart said, "Say hello."

I've written many others,
To help our story stay alive,
And, mend my healing heart,
With the hope it will survive.

I'm not sure how I will send them,
That's a puzzle to me now,
Maybe find an angel postman,
With a route that will allow.

If they come back, return to sender,
And, you're not receiving mail,
I'll accept your new conditions,
Allowing better judgment to prevail.

I still hope somehow they reach you,
But if not, I have another plan,
It may take a little longer,
And I'll deliver them by hand.

February 27, 2018

The First Visit

I saw you made a visit,
From the corner of my eye,
I felt your spirit's presence,
That my heart would not deny.

My awareness grew much stronger,
As I looked away, then back again,
Each time I sensed your gestures,
I knew it was you, my Adrianne.

Then I asked for reassurance,
With your appearance in my dreams,
To confirm this brief encounter,
I prayed my hopeful heart,
Had not fostered such extremes.

Then last night I was rewarded,
My first dream of you, my dear,
Just as I hoped and asked for,
You were standing oh so very near.

When I rushed toward you,
There were others in the way,
You appeared, for me, that was conclusive,
Then, I watched your image fade away.

I awoke, my heart fulfilled,
Now I know that you were here,
With patience, I will stand by
And wait for you to reappear.

March 1, 2018

One Season

Today the rain was slowly falling,
When I stopped to say hello,
It will melt your winter blanket,
And help the grass begin to grow.

I've read, the power of my thoughts,
Will help to draw you near,
I decided there's no better place,
To visit you than here.

Spring is right around the corner,
Just your shell is here I know,
I'll use this garden, for your memory,
For now, I have no better place to go.

Your new home, has just one season,
And it's resplendent year-round,
Where your presence adds fresh beauty,
To a land complete, and so profound.

When I leave behind, these earthly seasons,
I'll see, new lush gardens grow,
Feel the warmth of our reunion,
And together from above,
Watch the seasons change below.

March 5, 2018

Jim Is Home

Nine years ago today,
Adrianne's mother, Mary, passed away,
Mary's heart is filled with joy, to find,
That Jim came home to stay.

Her family keeps increasing,
And will through endless time,
One by one, she'll see them gather,
While serving God's design.

I saw Jim's star this morning,
Shine in brilliant blue,
With a gold one right beside him,
I knew his time on earth was through.

He will fill their days with laughter,
As he's been known to do,
And will help Adrianne and Mary,
Light a path for me and you.

March 7, 2018

Ode to Your Mother, Adrianne

Daylight days are longer now,
Soon the birds of spring will sing,
Returning from their winter homes,
Warm memories of you they bring.

The redbirds will be nesting,
On our entry door once more,
In the wreath you once provided,
Protected, like the year before.

They will raise a feathered family,
In the shelter you prepared,
Guard and nurture all their young ones,
Until their journey is declared.

I'm reminded of our children,
How you nourished every one,
Sacrifice with love not portioned,
From dawn till setting sun.

Like the birds outside our door,
You define His diagram,
You fostered your's delivered,
Adrianne, you epitomize God's plan.

March 10, 2018

A Time I Can't Rewrite

I find it hard to face tomorrow,
And another lonely night,
I can't find a way to let you go,
I'm clinging to a time, I can't rewrite.

Each night I close my eyes and pray,
You'll be in my dreams tonight,
Reliving all the love we shared,
Clinging to a time, I can't rewrite.

Clutching to your memory,
Even though you're out of sight,
This heart will not erase our love,
Always clinging to a time, I can't rewrite.

My heart's not absentminded,
And keeps yesterday held tight,
I'm left defenseless, and a prisoner,
While clinging to a time, I can't rewrite.

When nightfall brings another close,
I'll make believe and say good night,
Pretending you are here,
Still clinging to a time, I can't rewrite.

The day our souls are joined in heaven,
And Jesus says, all is right,
You'll be in my arms forever,
We will cling to a time, I can't rewrite.

March 11, 2018

I Can't Manage Yet

All I have now, are your pictures,
And memories I'll not forget,
I still break down, with no warning,
The loss of you, I can't manage yet.

There may come a time,
This heart of mine, someday will mend,
For now, teardrops fall with no regret,
Waiting on my heart to find an end.

Between now and someday,
My heart finds no safety net,
And without warning, tears start falling,
The loss of you, I can't manage yet,

Come with me, and dance down the hallway,
If only in my dreams,
It would soothe an empty feeling,
My heart knows, just what that means.

Once again, I'll be reminded,
Our first dance, and how we met,
Feel you glide across the hardwood,
The loss of you, I can't manage yet.

I don't know, what I'm looking for,
Or what I should expect,
This burden my heart carries,
At least for now, I can't protect.

March 14, 2018

Five Words

She said, "Come here, I love you,"
A gift my heart holds near,
While seated at her bedside,
From her loving voice so dear.

This special moment is recorded,
And replayed from time to time,
A memory I will treasure,
With many others all sublime.

Five words with countless value,
Stored in my mind and heart,
Spoken from a life in struggle,
This precious voice would soon depart.

Then Jesus said, "Come here, I love you,"
And he wiped this life away,
Five words returned as promised,
His eternal gift without decay.

I'll wait for Him to call me home,
In the meantime, I'll replay,
Five words, the gift she gave me,
She will repeat again someday.

March 16, 2018

His Helping Hand

The rest of my life here without you,
Seems, more than I can stand,
I long to see your smile once more,
Dance the hallway again, hand in hand.

We would make our way without music,
Just the words to an old country song,
It's a memory I still cling to,
I sang the tune, and you'd hum along.

Now, you're surrounded with music,
Singing angels give voice to the air,
Teaching the cherubs your dance step,
My absence my only despair.

My heart can't deny your arrival,
Your nowhere is somewhere I know,
In a beautiful home Jesus promised,
While His giving heart,
Helps my healing grow.

Recovery is far from completion,
Heartfelt memories ignore my command,
Tears still fall without warning,
For now, I need His helping hand.

March 19, 2018

A Dream of You

We walked together,
In a dream last night,
You kissed and held me tight,
Was this a visit from you?

A short but pleasant stroll,
Then you drifted out of sight,
Maybe you'll return tonight,
Was this a visit from you?

I'll be waiting for an encore,
It made my morning bright,
Will you come again tonight?
Please pardon me for asking,
Was this a visit from you?

My heart won't be discouraged,
When dawn brings the morning light,
With no dream of you in sight,
Please pardon me for asking,
Will I dream another visit from you?

March 20, 2018

Amen

When day is done, and I repose,
Fond thoughts of you invade,
Then restlessness comes over me,
But, sleep my heart won't trade.

Days weary weight takes over,
And wakefulness subsides,
My protective heart's diminished,
Our worlds again collide.

I'm delighted to find slumber,
Lucid dreams of you shine through,
For now, my only comfort,
While our worlds are split in two.

Someday we'll waltz with angels,
And I love you, is whispered again,
Tear drenched skies, will awaken rainbows,
Then, final words, from our Saviour,
Forever and ever, Amen.

March 21, 2018

Vicissitude

I've been called to change direction,
With whatever time is left,
My care for you, brought this about,
In your name, I'll do my best.

Reinvention, I'm no stranger,
Many times, my path has changed,
Assorted variations, required or invited,
Span over time a boundless range.

The lesson your needs taught me,
Brought new cause, to life's plan,
So your gift I'll carry forward,
Giving those in need a helping hand.

The seeds your life nourished,
Will be scattered, with you in mind,
And harvest, brighter days ahead,
For those confined or left behind.

And new friends that I encounter,
Will come to know, through you and me,
The life we shared, renewed my purpose,
Only Jesus could foresee.

March 22, 2018

Commitment

We loved to dance to country music,
Step for step our heart's entwined,
Familiar melodies, and love songs,
Memories forever on my mind.

I still listen to the music,
My dancing shoes will never hit the floor,
You're my one and only partner,
Our last dance, forever kept in store.

Shared vows I'll keep in order,
This heart will never have new space,
Dancing and romancing saved,
No one will ever take your place.

I long to hold you in my arms,
I will wait for your embrace,
Fill idle time with thoughts of you,
And, visualize the moment,
Meeting face-to-face.

I promise my committed love,
Will follow God's design,
And pray unwavered trust remains,
And, drifts somewhere between,
Your new world and mine.

March 24, 2018

With and Without

With and without you,
Your perpetual heartbeat brings you near,
Well composed in perfect rhythm,
With and without, I feel you here.

All the days, that I've shared with you,
Now escape the hands of time,
Our true love, without heartaches,
Again someday, will be combined.

When I get to where I'm going,
With our Savior's wounded hands,
Together, Father Time will tick forever,
Without the need, for the further plans.

I'll no longer be without you,
Tears I've shed will all be dried,
With the thankful wounds of Jesus,
With you again, I will reside.

March 26, 2018

Shadows of My Mind

I have a chamber in my heart,
Where you are stored forever,
And you're always in the
shadows of my mind.

Some days I feel your presence,
In our space, dividing your
new world and mine.
But whenever you are missing,
You're always in the
shadows of my mind.

I'm thankful you found comfort,
When you left this world behind,
Darling, it's selfish of me, but it's true,
I'm forever missing you,
And you're always in the
shadows of my mind.

This chamber in my heart,
Cries out, both night and day,
So whenever you can spare the time,
There's an open invitation,
And you're always welcome to invade the
shadows of my mind.

March 31, 2018

She Gave Her Son

That sun will soon be sinking,
Forecasts another lonely night,
A cold wind blows outside my door,
I foresee no change in sight.

The same wind blew three months ago,
Now I'm spending nights alone,
She flew away on angel wings,
To seek her peaceful home.

She found what Jesus promised,
Leaving me the pain He planned,
In return for her safe journey,
A price I pay by His command.

His sacrifice, gave pain to Mother Mary,
While scorned and scourged on the cross,
A greater sacrifice They made,
Our life's eternal at their cost.

Mary, please forgive me for lamenting,
The tears I shed cannot compare,
With all you suffered through the life He gave,
Now, my lost love has life immortal,
I too will be an heir.

April 2, 2018

Our Tapestry

The good Lord placed you in my way,
Knowing my life needed mending,
From the start you borrowed from my heart,
Your giving heart in need of lending.

I loaned my heart to you forever,
And you rendered all the mending,
You gave much more, than borrowed,
Now paid in full, no payment pending.

Our tapestry for life conceived,
Where love was always woven,
In panels of our hopes and dreams,
Weaving doors our love would open.

Always weaving, most times achieving,
Accepting pain in search of pleasure,
A panel for each boy we raised,
Your love for them, no need to measure.

He, who placed you in my way,
Knows my full life's still pending,
Our tapestry is not complete,
One panel left, for final mending.

April 4, 2018

The Opry

I wonder often, where we'd be,
If you, again, were here with me,
Many times, you spoke of Nashville,
And a visit to the Opry.

A longtime dream of yours,
I failed to make come true,
Now late for your forgiveness,
For many things I failed to do.

Our hearts someday, will meet again,
Another chance to do my part,
I promise I will be prepared,
My vow renewed, right from the start.

Wait for me, around the corner,
We will find that country show,
Meet and greet the stars in heaven,
Chasing dreams of long ago.

Finally sounds of Opry music,
Treasured voices pure and true,
Playing, singing all our love songs,
Your dream fulfilled from me to you.

April 7, 2018

One Step Behind

You're one step ahead of me for now,
Since you left my heart behind,
I'll catch up with you again someday,
When my life is reassigned.

I'm invited for a journey,
Departure time still in the air,
I know He'll keep His promise,
Your shining light will guide me there.

So, keep a pathway for me lighted,
And be waiting on that shore,
My wounded heart will travel with me,
Seeking hearts united, just like before.

From the darkness into sunshine,
Tears I shed will all be dried,
Our new chapter closed forever,
Pledged eternal side by side.

From there we'll step together,
No further need, to lag behind,
As promised, I'll catch up with you,
A gift from Jesus for all mankind.

April 9, 2018

A Stubborn Heart

I always have you on my mind,
Cause, my heart won't say goodbye,
It may seem to be a waste of time,
My doubting heart keeps asking, why?

Loving memories offer reasons,
A stubborn heart will not let die,
Collected from the day we met,
Treasured for a lifetime, is my hearts reply.

The remembrance of your laughter,
Is like music to my ear,
Mingled with a gracious smile,
A tender love I feel and hear.

Such memories are retraced each day,
With ease they reappear,
Our bygone days placed in my way,
And my heart claims, you are near.

This ailing heart, needs realignment,
All caused by you my dear,
If my mind neglects the love we shared,
My stubborn heart, will forever interfere.

April 13, 2018

Unrequited Love

No, you don't know how I feel,
Unless you travel in my shoes,
And someday, the time will come,
A time you can't refuse.

Your depth of love determines,
If you're walking in my shoes,
It will be precisely measured,
When you compare the love you chose.

So be prepared ahead of time,
Share all your love today,
This will help with later damage,
When your loved one goes away.

Your grief will be much greater,
If you fail to act today,
And recognize the gift you're given,
A steeper price you'll have to pay.

Profess each day the love you have,
No feelings left behind,
Purge all the love you've stored away,
Leaving nothing undefined.

So pay attention to my message,
Before you're called to lose,
Or you'll soon discover how I feel,
And be walking in my shoes.

April 16, 2018

Her Embers

You lit your flame within my heart
Many years ago,
Your love has fueled a lasting fire,
And the embers of your memory,
Now have eternal glow.

They will never be extinguished,
No need to reignite,
You stoked the flame with all your love,
Keeping embers burning bright.

You've touched the hearts of many,
Even some you never knew,
In poems they've come to know you,
In rhyme your love shines through.

The warmth your flames provided,
Leaves embers everywhere,
An everlasting gift from you,
For everyone to share.

April 18, 2018

When the Trumpet Blows

On the day when I'm called home,
Jesus said, you're waiting there,
Dreams and fantasies no longer,
Reliving all the love we share.

For now, my mind paints only pictures,
Of your laugh and precious smile,
And willing love surrendered,
That made my life worthwhile.

Perhaps, I'll meet you in a garden,
Where our loved ones tend to go,
We will greet and hug each other,
When I hear the trumpet blow.

My tears will flow like gutter rain,
When I touch that sacred ground,
Breathe the warmth of your sweet fragrance,
My waiting loved one finally found.

These are pictures for the moment,
And the timing is not clear,
When the ringing trumpet echoes,
My dear, your wait is over, this means that I am here.

April 19, 2018

Hide-and-Go-Seek

Hide and go seek, a childhood
game, from many years ago,
A game that I found fun to play,
And thought I would outgrow.

Now I'm searching for a place hide,
Seeking refuge for my heart,
And shelter all the tears I shed,
Each time I fall apart.

A temporary haven,
In case the teardrops start,
Find safety and protection,
And hide my wounded heart.

I seldom get a warning,
Or when it's time to play,
And hide myself from seekers,
When I need a hide away.

Then thoughts of you come creeping in,
And you come into view,
It's time to find a place to hide,
Or my feelings will show through.

Hide and go seek, is for children,
It's no longer fun to play,
Unless I am the seeker,
And, find your hiding place someday.

April 22, 2018

Strong Heart

You forgot many things,
Including my name,
But never forgot you loved me.

You told me so, in so many ways,
Your heart-filled eyes sent the message,
Replacing words you no longer could raise.

Your heart still owned a memory,
Sharing love, stored over time,
With a special way of expressing,
Understood from your heart to mine.

Hearts are stronger than minds,
Stride for stride minds often lose pace,
Your loving heart had momentum,
A picture with no empty space.

Your heart never gave into the notion,
Through your struggle it couldn't revive,
You more than proved it was worthy,
And your hearts strong memory survived.

Now you are restored in heaven,
Mending a worn out mind,
Repairing whatever was needed,
Your strong heart, as always, still mine.

April 23, 2018

What Am I Going to Do Tonight?

Today I'm here alone without you,
Thinking of you again,
But what am I going to do tonight?

No one to turn to or say good night,
And when daylight comes tomorrow,
Rain or shine I'll be all right,
But what am I going to do tonight?

Maybe a dream, with you in fading sight,
Then I'll wait the start of a new day,
And hope, today's future is bright,
But what am I going to do tonight?

Pretend for the moment, when we reunite,
Then the day begins without you,
Knowing the past I can't rewrite,
But what am I going to do tonight?

Life is not the same without you,
I find it hard to meet the change,
I know I can't give up the fight,
Though each evening leaves me wondering,
What am I going to do tonight?

April 23, 2018

You and I

When I hear our favorite songs,
With closed eyes, I pretend,
You are in my arms once more,
And dancing together again.

The songs are pleasant reminders,
Of when and how we met,
A time I'll cherish forever
A time I'll not forget.

Now the lyrics from "We Could,"
Often bring teardrops to my eyes.

"If anyone could find the joy
that true love brings a girl
and boy, we could, we could
you and I."

A song we danced to many times,
And will always stand the test,
The same song played with tear-filled eyes,
When you were laid to rest.

"If anyone could pray each night
And thank the Lord that all is right,
we could, darling, we could
you and I."

April 27, 2018

Therapy

When I dream of you at night,
I always wake up smiling,
And make believe that you
Were passing through.

It helps hold my life together,
As strange as that may seem,
But it offers hopeful comfort,
When I see you in my dreams.

Though you never say a word,
You're still passing through my heart,
Leaving footprints of your memory,
Relieving pain while we're apart.

My dreams of you serve purpose,
They engender for a time,
A needed pause for healing,
When your soothing heart engages mine.

So I'm waiting for your therapy,
And you've been missing for a while,
Please meet me in a dream again,
And I'll awaken with a smile.

April 28, 2018

Proclamation

Darling, I don't know when,
But, Jesus promised someday
We'll be together again.

Your portraits hanging in my mind,
A smile forever stored away,
Not one memory left behind,
The reflection of your beauty on display.

Someday He'll change the picture,
And remove it from the frame,
Repaint our lives from scripture,
A prophetic promise then proclaimed.

I'll see our loved ones all around,
Through the glimmer of new light,
All those missing finally found,
Darker days are now made bright.

With our families now all gathered,
I will see my Mom and Dad,
Spend endless time together,
Turn back pages we once had.

The day my dark clouds gather,
And the cold winds cross the land,
We'll be hand in hand with Jesus,
He'll have carried out His plan.

April 30, 2018

Had I Been the First to Go

Her life with special meaning,
Defined my path, and made me grow,
A privilege I'd be missing
Had I been the first to go.

Her love was my possession,
Her needs I learned to know,
A chance I may have failed to meet
Had I been the first to go.

Had I been the first to go,
I wouldn't have this pain today,
But, the pain my heart traded for
Took my loved one's pain away.

The gift that her life taught me,
Was the plan for me to stay,
To prepare her for her journey
And help ease her on the way.

Had I been the first to go,
Leaving her the price to pay,
She would've welcomed His intended plan
And served until my final day.

May 2, 2018

The Veil

A veil now stands between us,
A veil I can't see through,
Somehow when I am dreaming,
You're out of reach,
But nearly in my view.

My faith alone will thin this veil,
Thoughts and love will bring you near,
Some night, your presence will prevail,
Through the veil you will appear.

This moment will be treasured,
And lead me from my world of gloom,
It will feed and heal a wounded heart,
Providing all it can consume.

Picking up the shattered pieces,
Of your loss left at our door,
This battered heart, although splintered,
Does not forget what's gone before.

The veil that stands between us,
Needs some thinning at this time,
So you can step in closer
And relieve this wounded heart of mine.

May 9, 2018

Forever Is Longer than Before"

The one thing I depend on is,
Forever is longer than before.

I won't forget one yesterday,
They bring back memories I hold dear,
Collected in a lifetime,
Through our years together dear.

As I ponder days remembered,
They've escaped the hands of time,
Befores all moved by quickly,
Through our lifetime, yours and mine.

When befores are all assembled,
And measured over time,
They count, and are recorded,
But, leave a mountain yet to climb.

The befores are now behind us,
They afford a shorter time,
The mountain tops forever,
Where the lights of heaven shine.

It's here we meet our Savior,
With His welcome open door,
And chose together now forever,
It's much longer than before.

May 10, 2018

You Can't Be Replaced

No one knows how much I miss you,
Nor, can one feel this heart of mine,
They would need to know the history,
And, why our hearts were so entwined.

Both you and I, we know the reason,
You were there when most required,
With support and understanding,
Leaving nothing more, to be desired.

I disclosed my deepest feelings,
You trusted me, and did the same,
Nothing hidden all discovered,
Rings exchanged, you took my name.

Our hearts were kindled from the start,
You recognized my quirks and flaws,
When discouraged you encouraged,
Growing love without a pause.

We shared our love without conditions,
Learn to give each other space,
All disputes and disagreements,
Soon were gone without a trace.

I thank the Lord,
He made sure I found you,
Your love and loss can't be replaced.

May 11, 2018

Under Cover

I can't adjust to spending nights alone,
Or crying myself to sleep,
The only thing I'm thankful for
There's no one here to see me weep.

I still say our nightly prayer,
Just like we did before,
Sometimes pretending she's still here,
And, I reach for her once more.

I find the pillow empty,
That should be of no surprise,
But, my imagination wanders,
And, she's here through tear drenched eyes.

I can hear her softly breathing,
Her sweet fragrance fills the air,
Then a glimpse of my surroundings,
Once again the pillows bare.

No one here to see me weeping,
Or to question my welfare,
And, deprive me of a moment,
Of a time we once shared.

These nights alone, provide me cover,
I can let my heart unwind,
Keep tender feelings undiscovered,
All dreams and fantasies are mine.

May 16, 2018

A Thousand Times a Day

My mind is occupied with thoughts of you,
A thousand times a day,
It makes no difference what I'm doing,
Thoughts of you are in my way.

I can't separate or filter out,
The other things I need to do,
With a mind filled a thousand times,
And overwhelmed with thoughts of you.

I know the underlying problem,
It's all directed by my heart,
Guiding memories by the thousands,
A source I'm unable to outsmart.

The memories my heart feeds my mind,
A thousand times a day,
Are worthy of remembrance,
And they're safely stored away.

Coping with these interruptions,
A thousand times a day,
There is a chance. I'll find the time,
for the other things, but probably not today.

May 19, 2018

You Were My Gift

When my mind begins to wander,
And I recall the days gone by,
I can't help but ask the question,
How would life have been without you,
And the change your love supplied?

You were a gift to me from heaven,
When my life was upside down,
Struggling down an aimless pathway,
And you turned my life around.

I was slow to meet, the change you offered,
You risked your heart with no protection,
Giving time for new direction,
And my addiction turned around,
Because of your affection.

My promised vows now reconsidered,
A child conceived help made the change,
You blessed my life, with resurrection
And another need to rearrange.

The question asked, still begs an answer,
Without you, where would I be?
I only know, I'm forever thankful,
You were my love,
God's gift to me.

May 21, 2018

Sharing Despair

I'm trying to find somewhere safe,
A place to heal my weary heart,
And hold my life together,
Find some room for joy to start.

Maybe find another lonely soul,
Who's as miserable as me,
And do for one another,
While sharing common misery.

Share the burden of our loss,
With no intention to replace,
Simply manage over time, the memories,
That our hearts cannot erase.

Shed a healing beam of sunlight,
When darkened days are dim,
Feel free, recount our stories,
Instead of holding them within.

I'm not searching for new romance,
Just a buffer zone if found,
It may ease the pain I'm living,
It may turn two lives around.

If God has this, in His plan,
And He assigns someone to me,
We will carry out His purpose,
And mend each other's misery.

May 25, 2018

Empty Nest

The redbirds failed to make their nest,
Outside our door this year,
Someone may have told them
That you're no longer here.

The wreath that you provided,
Hangs empty on our door,
A safe place for their nesting,
Last year, and years before.

Their absence makes me wonder,
Did you ask, if they'd come too?
It's strange you both are missing,
Did they fly away with you?

If I could fly like redbirds,
I'd be at your waiting door,
And wrap you in a feathered nest,
And hold you close once more.

No, I can't fly, but angels can,
Someday, I'll catch a ride with them,
And with the missing redbirds,
You'll be in my arms again.

Back in my arms forever,
Forever from this day,
And like the faithful redbirds,
We'll build a nest that's here to stay.

May 27, 2018

Pictures

Her pictures are stained from teardrops,
But there are others in my mind,
Saved with full protection,
And will stand the test of time.

They appear in perfect focus,
Filtered through these tears of mine,
Her picture panorama,
A view of treasures left behind.

There's no need to even close my eyes,
To see her smiling face,
Pictures draped with memories,
One by one, pass clearly into place.

With each picture I'm reminded,
Of her beauty, style, and grace,
Her complexion with perfection,
Time and age would not erase.

These pictures, capture God's creation,
And record the days gone by,
They'll be stored away forever,
And bring cause for me to cry.

May 29, 2018

Broken in Two

My heart's no longer breaking,
'Cause I heard it break in two,
Divided helpless without protection,
This broken heart I can't renew.

Two parts both in confusion,
One-half won't say farewell,
The other tired and weary,
Yet together they must dwell.

Mornings leave me wondering,
What the day will have in store,
Will it be another day of gloom?
Like so many days before.

I'd look forward to tomorrow,
If I were offered yesterday,
Bring my heart back in reunion,
But, the past will not replay.

Then nightfall gives no cover,
My heart feels the lasting strain,
Even though they are divided,
Both parts remain in pain.

Today, I'll start the morning different,
Than I did the day before,
Give my heart a special treatment,
And, for a moment, make believe,
She comes walking through the door.

June 7, 2018

Our Love Story

Our love story's never ending,
Though you're gone, our story's not complete,
While another chapters pending,
Our hearts have never missed a beat.

Some days I feel your presence,
My heart imagines you are near,
Recalls the beauty of your essence,
The memories pass by crystal clear.

Our hearts, will always beat together,
And survive through endless time,
We have battled stormy weather,
There'll come a day, the sun will shine.

When Jesus writes the other chapter,
Our love story will not rest,
We will walk within the rapture,
When our story, He has blessed.

And, without end,
Our love story will go on,
Eternal in His promised place,
Together, like we've dreamed of, for so long.

June 9, 2018

A Movie Interruption

When my mind is filled with other things,
Her memory still shows up,
Closing in on me, without a warning,
And my fragile heart and mind link up.

Then treasured moments, cross a silver screen,
A motion picture on review,
I'm captured by the leading lady,
As she glides smoothly into view.

So well I know the part she played,
It's embedded in my heart,
A devoted wife and mother,
And love, she was willing to impart.

A love revealed in countless ways,
Unselfish to the core,
A mother, brother, or child in need,
Her heart, swung an open door.

The part she played can't be replaced,
No stand-in will suffice,
Her starring role is beyond reach,
No one can match her value, or the price.

Now, through blurry eyes, I realize,
I've seen this movie, many times before,
Then her pleasant interruption fades,
And it's back to other things once more.

June 13, 2018

Family Reunion

I stopped by the cemetery,
As I traveled on my way,
To a family reunion, and
I took some time to pray,
With some loved ones who are missing,
And won't be here today.

The family names recorded,
Hung on long scrolls today,
Many assembled in reunion,
And names of those who passed away.

The next reunion I engage,
My wife and parents will be there,
Waiting my reunion,
No more longing or despair.

A reunion we all dream of,
Unlike we've gathered here below,
The one He promised up above,
Where the lights of heaven shimmer,
And His angels soar with love.

All reunions in the future,
Or planned down here below,
Some assembled here today,
Will be among the missing, on the scroll.

But there's a grand reunion waiting,
With those missing up above,
If you believe in Jesus,
And His everlasting love.

So, commit your heart and soul,
Fore your name's forever written,
On our Shepherd's final scroll.

June 16, 2018

The Golden Years

The garden where you're resting,
Was freshly mowed today,
Dew glistens on the flowers,
A breeze softly whispers you're okay.

The golden years together,
Interwoven, we still share,
Our love's collected in this garden,
When I join with you in prayer.

Today the sun is shining,
Clouds are few, it's mostly clear,
So wrap me in your spirit,
And you'll see me standing here.

I wait to feel your presence,
Though, through the veil I cannot see,
While praying in this garden,
You have a better view than me.

You have more than earned my visits,
And my attempt to animate,
A lifetime we are missing,
Only He can replicate.

Our true golden years are waiting,
And together, we will reclaim,
When I find you in His garden,
On the day you call my name.

June 21, 2018

Six Months Ago, Today

Six months ago, today,
I buried yesterday and tomorrow,
Time ran out, none left to borrow,
Leaving memories, pain, and sorrow.

Precious memories were not buried,
They're what's left of yesterday,
Six months is insufficient,
Tomorrow adds more pain each day.

It's hard to face tomorrow,
With yesterday so close behind,
The time together, that we borrowed,
Lingers on my heart and mind.

Rain or shine I stop to visit,
And say a prayer each day,
A tomorrow peaceful moment,
My prayer of thanks for yesterday.

Tomorrows will continue,
So will thoughts of yesterday,
Six more months won't be sufficient,
My pain and sorrows here to stay.

I'd find future in tomorrow,
If I could borrow yesterday
Or when I awaken her some morning,
With a lasting smile someday.

June 25, 2018

He Has a Plan

My heart won't let you go,
It has a memory of its own,
I try to help it understand,
We won't always be alone,
Our Shepherd has a welcome plan,
And we'll be led to your new home.

I told my heart, you're waiting there,
And, we can leave the past behind,
No longer dwell on memories,
Or turning pages back in time.

We will never be alone again,
When we're joined together there,
Exploring, heaven's hills and valleys,
Embrace your tender, loving care.

But for now my heart still wanders,
And, falls back to days gone by,
Relying on your memories,
Though, broke no promise, it would try.

So I told my heart, the next time,
we look behind, remember,
Objects in the mirror,
Are closer than they appear,
Please try and understand,
It takes time to heal a broken heart,
Have faith, and trust He has a plan.

June 27, 2018

When The Bells Of Heaven Toll

At the bottom of the stairs,
Just inside the door,
I see you smiling up at me,
Like so many times before.

Are you coming home or leaving?
I can't tell, the impressions not complete,
Your smiling image has no motion
Then fades away before we meet.

Imaginary visions bring me comfort,
Keeping future dreams alive,
A reminder, and precursor,
Our love as promised will survive.

Such harbingers are welcomed,
With my present state of mind,
They send a hopeful message,
Without conditions or deadline.

I'm not privy to a timeframe,
The schedules out of my control,
But, you'll never disappear again,
I'll recapture you forever
When the bells of Heaven toll.

June 27, 2018

Did You Try to Make a Difference?

Did you take some time to pray,
For the frail old couple, you saw today?
To help them on their journey,
One may be not far away.

Did you try to make a difference,
In someone's life today?

And the poor soul on the corner,
With a cardboard sign that reads, homeless,
Did you doubt his intention or question his needs,
As you passed him on your way?

And the aged woman at the grocery store,
Struggling, with a heavy shopping load,
Overburdened with limbs now slowed.
Did you offer a hand, and see her on her way?

Did you try to make a difference,
In someone's life today?

Did you befriend a disappointed child,
And brighten up his day,
With support and interaction,
Allowing cares to drift away?

Did you try to make a difference,
In someone's life today?
Or fail the eyes of your giving heart
And simply hurry on your way.

July 1, 2018

The Puzzle

My life is now in pieces,
Like puzzle parts
A child at play spread out,
I'm left to solve the puzzle
Of a life now scrambled all about.

The puzzle parts are fragments
From my world turned upside down,
I'm gathering fractured remnants,
Most are missing, some I've found.

I can't replace the missing pieces
That match the few I may discover,
And the reason they are missing
Keeps me searching, trying to recover.

There is no model or new pattern,
In spite of my resolve,
To put this puzzle back together,
It's not meant for me to solve.

Someday, missing parts will find their place,
As well as those I've found,
When the Creator of this mystery puzzle
Rearranges all the pieces,
And decides its time and chooses,
To turn my world around.

July 6, 2018

I Believe

My love for you keeps growing,
And will forevermore,
That's the way He planned it,
You were my gift He had in store.

In the meantime, you are missing,
Because Jesus loves you too,
He reunited you with loved ones,
A gift our Savior promised you.

The Teacher taught me how to love you,
I learned all the reasons why,
So my love will last forever,
There's no need to say goodbye.

Our parting is a passing,
A temporary shift in time,
Intended for the faithful,
And our Savior's grand design.

Someday we'll share salvation,
You'll no longer be my absentee,
He once blessed me with your love,
A gift I wasn't able to foresee,
But now, I believe the Giver,
Has saved another gift for me.

July 8, 2018

You Won't Be Missing Anymore

You are missed today, yesterday,
And the day before,
And I'll miss you tomorrow,
And all the days remaining,
I have left to borrow.

When I run out of borrowed time,
I'll be on the Jordan, in a boat with angels,
And I'll come sailing on my way,
Morning, noon, or late at night,
You won't be missed another day.

Your missing days are numbered,
And I'll count them one by one,
My restless heart will wait each day,
From dawn to setting sun.

Waiting alone was not my choice,
But I'll not forsake His plan,
The numbered days will sail their course,
Because I trust the Anchorman.

He's the Captain of the boat,
I won't be sailing all alone,
When the numbered days have counted down,
We'll sail to your new home.

He'll drop the anchor at your door,
And you won't be missing anymore.

July 11, 2018

One Is Half of Two

I knew the day was coming,
And I promised to be strong,
For the Holy Spirit's final visit,
Then I discovered I was wrong.

My future dreams all crumbled,
A precious soul plucked from the room,
My heart wilted like a flower,
Never more to grow or bloom.

My angel left our home with angels,
I felt my heart had tagged along,
I found it later lying emptied,
Once again, I was wrong.

She was heaven-bound without me,
I would have gladly gone along,
Now I'm living life without her,
And without her I'm not strong.

They say there's strength in numbers,
And I know that to be true,
She made us strong together,
Fore two is more than one,
Now I am one, the lonely half of two.

July 15, 2018

It Only Takes a Heart

When you're called to recognize a need,
With compassion do your part,
For a friend, a loved one, or a stranger,
It only takes a heart.

I know where I'm coming from,
Because I know where I've been,
And the Lord only knows where I'd be,
Without the heart of a mother, a father,
Sisters and brothers or a friend,
It only takes a heart.

We were created as God's children,
And our strands aren't for apart,
Bound and joined, to toil together,
Changing hard times for good times,
It only takes a heart.

So bring some sunshine to another,
With nothing more than your heart,
Thank the Good Lord for your blessings,
Take your turn, and be a steward,
He will show you where to start,
It only takes a heart.

July 22, 2018

A Lullaby

When awake or when I'm dreaming,
Your sweet presence fills the air,
A passing fragrance well remembered,
A soothing breeze for my despair.

Then, I wait for you to whisper,
"There you are," like many times before,
With a tear, I softly answer, "Here I am,"
A wishful dream, then nothing more.

At bedtime, there you are again,
I hear you breathing next to me,
Each breath is like a melody,
A lullaby to set cares free.

As a child, my Mother sang to me,
Tura Lura Lura, an Irish lullaby,
The melody you bring each night,
I'm reminded, hush now don't you cry.

Your heartful melody, is a remedy,
Though I'm not a child today,
It's not fantasy or make-believe,
I know you meet me here each day.

So sing me off to sleep tonight,
With your familiar lullaby,
And whisper to me, on the final verse,
Hush now don't you cry.

July 26, 2018

Yes, You're Missed

Not a day goes by that I don't wonder,
If you really know, how much you're missed,
Can you see me when I'm crying,
Every time your picture's kissed?

When I'm recalling lasting memories,
Do you share those times with me,
Reliving special moments,
Are you near enough to hear or see?

Are you waiting in your garden,
When I stop by to pray?
To let you know I miss you,
I make a visit every day.

Can you see me in this empty home,
Where you're missed forevermore,
And feel the looming sadness,
Each time I close the door?

With faith I'll go on wondering,
I'll say a prayer each night,
That your heart is always reaching,
And you're only out of sight.

July 29, 2018

Lasting Love

Someday, my broken heart will mend,
The day my Savior calls me home,
She'll beckon with a smile and wave,
I am here, never more to be alone.

I'll embrace my missing darling,
She's the one I've longed to see,
I'll be shedding tears of joy,
When I see her gently come to me.

While waiting, I can see her now,
Who could forget, her smile and grace,
As she leads me down a golden path,
I can hear her saying softly,
"You have found our final place."

Then she guides me through a garden,
Beside a peaceful flowing stream,
With fountains, brooks, and flowers,
One, seen often in my dreams,

I'll gaze upon the one I love,
With all the love I have in store,
A broken heart now mended,
Side by side forevermore.

Our lasting love as He decreed,
Together, just like we were before.

July 30, 2018

All Because of You

They say, "Absence makes the heart grow fonder."
I know this to be true,
My heart was always full of love,
And keeps growing now, all because of you.

This heart has no room for new love,
That wouldn't work, because of you,
I'll carry on like you're still here,
Turn back time, when our love was new.

I'll feed my heart those memories,
That's what I'm meant to do,
The treasured moments left behind,
Will fill the lonely days and nights,
All because of you.

Because of you, another's heart could not prevail,
My heart's standing in the way,
A heart, still growing fonder,
And will, until they carry me away.

Life has taught me many lessons,
I've learned, what I can, and cannot do,
And, I know, I'll never love again,
All because of you.

August 2, 2018

Your Laugh and Smile

The memory of your laugh and smile,
And the way you warmed a room,
A picture often turned to,
To ease my days of gloom.

Recalling smiling pictures,
Lingering in my heart and mind,
They soothe the lonely moments,
That occur from time to time.

Your smile was always special,
You touched so many hearts,
The returning smiles, from little children,
Who sensed the love your smile imparts.

An infectious smile and laughter,
A forever memory held within,
If only I could wind your picture up,
And hear your easy laugh again.

My life would be in shambles,
Without the memory of your smile,
And someday we'll laugh together,
I'll be waiting, it may take a little while.

Then you'll share with me forever,
Your treasured laugh and smile.

August 22, 2018

I Will Follow

I keep holding on to memories,
Held in my heart and mind,
They visit me both night and day,
Laced in love you left behind.

Reoccurring without notice,
Reminding me I'm left alone,
Recapturing the love we shared,
Then, I save my sorrow in a poem.

Without you, my spirit's down,
Though thankful I'm still around,
Nonetheless, ready and waiting,
For the day I am heaven-bound.

I will gladly leave this world behind,
When our Savior calls my name,
I'll keep searching for new meaning,
Without you, life is not the same.

Since you left our home for heaven,
Heaven, is where I want to be,
I trust His promise, you're waiting there,
Don't give up on me,
I will follow,
It's you I long to see.

August 27, 2018

Homesick

When I come home, I'm still homesick,
It's not the home it was before,
Lights are out, no smell of supper,
No one greets me at the door.

No hello, I'm met with silence,
She's not here waiting, like before,
A home once difficult to leave,
It's not easy to return here anymore.

The only thing that breaks the silence,
Is the closing of the door,
And I'm reminded once again,
What homesick has in store.

Then I go from room to room,
I see her pictures everywhere,
And the memory of her absence,
Only adds to my despair.

This empty home leaves me homesick,
No change each day, when I return,
Enduring walls surrounding me,
Can't speak or offer some concern.

But I know Jesus spoke,
I will count on His assurance,
There's a home for me in heaven,
She's waiting to greet me at the door,
I'll never be homesick anymore.

September 1, 2018

Our Domain

When I lay down my weary head,
And close my eyes, my heart says let's pretend,
She's snuggled here beside me,
A notion, I'm not able to defend.

Like a child, I succumb to make believe,
My imagination brings her near,
A memory magnified, a thousand times,
Then, with opened eyes she disappears.

The end is disappointing,
A moment short, for a memory so clear,
Future visits will not be this brief,
And open eyes won't interfere.

From now on, when I reach bedtime,
I'll listen, and pay attention to my heart,
Introducing timeless memories,
Believing, two souls aren't far apart.

With closed eyes, I'll drift off to sleep,
The chosen memory will remain,
I'll not risk an open eye till sun up,
When her spirits home, in our domain.

September 7, 2018

Disregard The Weather

Today the sun is shining,
The sky is milky blue,
No clouds in sight, they're missing,
And I'm reminded, so are you.

The sky may change tomorrow,
When returning clouds come into view,
Unlike the clouds, you'll not return,
But, I'll feel your presence passing through.

I can't predict the changing weather,
I can predict no change in you,
The lingering presence, you left behind,
A purposeful reminder, of a love so true.

From the beginning to the end,
Like Jesus, I can always count on you,
Sunny days or cloudy skies,
Somehow, your love comes shining through.

You keep spreading love, and reassurance
For those who wait their time,
Your frequent presence sends a message,
Disregard the weather, someday you'll greet,
All the loved ones left behind.

September 9th, 2018

Gratitude

Though, our tomorrow didn't come,
You left knowing that I love you,
I reminded you in many ways,
And your eyes, told me that you knew,
With a smile, those same brown eyes
would often say, I love you too.

When words were hard to come by,
From a voice no longer clear,
Your love so pure but quiet,
Always brought about a tear.

Spoken words were not required,
To touch this heart of mine,
Those eyes that cast a loving glance,
Alone, will keep our hearts entwined.

Our tomorrows have been set aside,
He promised, they'll be renewed,
Someday begin, where we left off,
With abounding gratitude.

Gratitude, for the love we share,
Gratitude, for the life He gave,
And grateful, He rose from the grave,
Our souls, and new tomorrows are forever saved.

September 12, 2018

You Were The Answer

The day my eyes fell upon you,
You were woven in my heart,
Then a voice spoke out of silence
She's a prenuptial state of art.

I heard direction in that moment,
My assignment was made clear,
And I embarked on a mission,
To capture you my dear.

With weeks of dedication,
I never wavered from resolve,
My intention had a purpose,
Up till now my life had stalled.

I knew you were the answer,
Someone special told me so,
You were sent, to turn a life around,
For someone, you didn't know.

Then one evening I decided,
To finally take a chance,
Risking you would turn me down,
I asked you for a dance.

Your acceptance was our beginning,
Only He could orchestrate,
His prenuptial recognition,
We would later celebrate.

September 15, 2018

Your Hand In Mine

While living on memories,
Nurtured in my heart and mind,
I'm reminded, of the distance
we traveled, together over time.
A road with turns and bends,
And sometimes hills to climb.

We supported one another,
As we journeyed day to day,
avoiding ruts along the way,
And, when hills were hard to climb,
I could always find, your hand in mine.

Sunny days or rainy days,
When skies weren't always blue,
I've said before, and I'll say again,
No matter, I could always count on you.

But, now when storm clouds gather,
And I'm alone without my bride,
Storms with raindrops bring teardrops,
With you no longer by my side.

I'll keep counting on you,
And I'm waiting for the time,
When, I wake up and find,
Once again, your hand in mine.

September 16, 2018

Here I Am Again

I was blessed for more than "50" years,
Because of you my loving bride,
And now I have a problem
I can't turn those years aside.

When I come by each day
to say hello, and say a prayer,
And, I pause to hear you whisper,
"There you are"
I sense you see me standing there.

Your whisper could be from the wind,
Or simply what I chose to hear,
I feel a presence speaking to me,
Your picture in my mind is clear.

It may be wishful thinking,
And it could be make believe,
I don't question why He sends me,
Cause, there's fulfillment when I leave.

He has a purpose for my visits,
I'll trust, and follow unaware,
So it's, here I am again tomorrow,
When I stop by to say a prayer.

September 20, 2018

What True Love Means

Thank the Lord, you were my blessing,
I really needed you, and the love
you gave so free,
Then He blessed me with another gift,
He said, now you're in need of me.

A chance for me to earn your love,
At first, I didn't understand,
Then over time your needs developed,
I realized my purpose, and
the perfection of His plan.

It was now my turn, to
repay your love,
And be as needed by your side,
He assured me not to worry,
If I tired, He would hold me up,
He would teach and be my guide.

I learned what true love really means,
As I cared for you each day,
While sharing cherished moments,
With more love than words can say.

So, with His help, and trust,
I returned love held within,
Though you're gone, true love keeps growing,
I'm thankful for His gift and you,
I wish, I could do it all over again.

September 23, 2018

We Will Dance In Heaven

I was attracted to you,
Like a bee to a hive,
At a time, seeking someone,
To rekindle my life, keeping passion alive.

My heart knew, when I first saw you,
There was no need, to search anymore,
And our love was launched forever,
When we met on the hardwood floor.

Now, when I hear an old Country song,
I remember that time, and pretend,
You're back once more, in my loving arms,
And we're dancing together again.

Play me some more Country music,
So this memory can last until dawn,
I'll hold you closer than ever,
While we dance to your favorite songs.

When the music dims fading slowly,
A host of angels dance you away,
A shift from my arms for the meantime,
Until we dance in Heaven someday.

September 26, 2018

Piecing Things Together

Piecing things together,
Is not an easy thing to do,
Because I live on memories,
They bring loving thoughts of you.

I try holding life together,
But, my heart won't say goodbye,
Each time a yesterday's recalled,
I wipe a teardrop from my eye.

You're the missing piece I can't replace,
Though your memory's here to stay,
I'll carry on, a day at a time,
But, your painful loss won't go away.

You may be gone, but not forever,
My heart knows right where you are,
He, will reassemble the missing pieces,
And lead me to your shining star.

Piecing things together,
Is easy for Jesus to do,
Memories and yesterday's, no longer needed,
When, He rejoins me with you.

September 29, 2018

When I Wake Up With You

Each morning surrounds an empty hollow,
Only hopeful dreams come passing through,
I keep waiting to begin a day,
When I wake up, and I'm with you.

A new beginning with no ending,
I trust His promise to be true,
With faith, I'm waiting for the day,
When I wake up, and I'm with you.

The empty hollow, again refilled,
With the love we always knew,
A morning with a lasting glow,
When I wake up, and I'm with you.

My dreams, once only hopeful,
Will become, someday past due,
I'll be surrounded by your love again,
When I wake up, and I'm with you.

When I wake up with you,
And see the smile,
That warms my heart once more,
We will awaken together forever,
When I reach that distant shore.

October 3, 2018

I'm Not The Poet

I pen lyrics from my heart,
I'm not a poet by design,
Just a heart, speaking in a way,
That offers comfort for my mind.

A mind wandering with memories,
It takes no talent on my part,
They're treasures of a lifetime, stored,
A gift He gave, to a tender heart.

A window opened to my soul,
A need, only He could see,
The emotions, He directs in verse,
Are heartfelt love, for therapy.

Favorite memories right from the heart,
Reminders, to soften and mend the mind,
Overheard by loved ones lost,
From me, and others left behind.

Now, every time a story's shared,
Our love and thoughts pass on,
They ease a mind, and warm a heart,
And bring a smile to those beyond.

October 4, 2018

Her Footsteps

When I come home, to this empty house,
I pause, before I close the door,
And imagine for a moment,
I hear her footsteps once more.

A familiar voice calls out, is that you?
And I say yes, it's me my dear,
When I close the door, and turn,
I find only me, no one else is here.

Her voice that echoed in the past,
And her footsteps disappear,
A home still cold and empty,
Just a memory, when she was here.

If I could find my way back,
To a time when she was here,
I'd trade today, and tomorrow,
To hear those footsteps reappear.

With a voice so sweet and mellow,
Falling gently on my ear,
In rhythm with each footstep,
And each footstep brings her near.

I know the day is coming,
When she'll call to me once more,
And again, I'll hear her footsteps
Like so many times before.

October 7, 2018

Do Mothers Cry In Heaven

Does a Mother cry in Heaven
When there's sadness here below?
Or does He shield, and protect her,
From things to sad for her to know?

Does the pain one cause or feel
Reflect, back to her somehow?
When we make mistakes and stumble,
Can she see, will He allow?

But if the veil, is a one-way mirror,
And everything's in sight,
There's a Mother up in Heaven,
Crying for her son tonight.

She'll pray for angels to protect him,
And remind him in a dream,
Life's a gift, let it flow and grow,
God plans a natural way to Heaven,
When it's your turn, He'll let you know.

October 8, 2018

Our Sacred Bond

For the present my life is empty,
Though the future glimmers bright,
My mind stays flooded with His promise,
I keep holding on, both day and night.

I know someday I'll be with you,
I'll live that dream, until it's true,
When, I lay down my weary head,
The last thought on my mind is you.

I have always been a dreamer,
And, I've realized a few,
But none were as important,
As my dream of loving you,
You were my dream come true.

My grief, and sorrow can be measured,
By the depth of love for you,
Deeper the love, deeper the sorrow,
My heart tells me this is true.

I trust, sorrow will be swept away
When I reach the far beyond,
I'll be guided there by angels,
With joy, He'll renew our sacred bond.

October 18, 2018

Painting Pictures

There is an easel in my mind.
On which, I'm painting pictures.
Painting pictures of the splendor waiting me,
When I'm gathered up by angels,
And, greeted by the Man from Galilee.

My mind can't capture, or imagine,
All the wonders I will see,
But there's one vivid picture,
I know you're waiting there for me.

I wasn't by your side, to say goodbye,
A picture, lingering on my heart and mind.
When, our forever picture's painted,
I can leave that picture far behind.

While painting pictures of Heaven,
From a model I can't see,
I'll trust on faith and lessons taught,
His gift, I hold inside me.

So, my canvas, is filled with
flowers, brooks, and fountains,
And as far as one can see,
Angels, surrounding all our loved ones,
Our Saviour's promise with love eternally.

October 21, 2018

Climate Change

There is a sadness in my heart,
That too often brings a tear,
Then I wipe my eyes and cover up,
And hope those feelings disappear.

Tears fall without a warning,
Because of sadness they're in season,
Like falling leaves from autumn trees,
The climate change provides the reason.

Each year four seasons are expected,
Neither climate is the same,
Sadness, a climate you left behind,
A condition without change.

I believe, change awaits in Heaven,
Where sadness can't be found,
Nor tears like leaves from autumn trees,
Just you, to wrap my arms around.

My sadness is doomed forever,
Heaven has a single lasting season,
All tears, will be tears of joy,
Our Saviour's promise is the reason.

October 25, 2018

Division

When I see an older couple,
Still together, with age and graying hair.
Aiding each other on their journey,
I pause, and say a prayer.

I ask forgiveness for my selfish thought,
Wishing we were in their place,
A moments envy, with no intention,
Of depriving them His grace.

Someday in time they will divide,
Just, like you and me,
So, my prayer for them,
Is for here and, then,
Their future, He will decree.

One will be called, the one left behind,
Will be tracing back in time,
When they walked hand in hand together,
A memory framed forever in the mind.

In a new world, with life renewed,
Again, their loving bond will dominate,
Until then, the one remaining,
Like me will have to wait.

October 26, 2018

When You Wave

From a balcony in Heaven,
Someday, you'll wave to me,
A vision I have safely stored,
A desire I trust, and plainly see.

An image I will not erase,
Until my mission is complete,
When you see me smiling just below
with tears of thankful joy,
Bowed kneeling, at our Saviour's feet.

Escorted by a host of angels,
The golden stairway I'll ascend,
And, meet you at the crown of Heaven,
A new beginning with no end.

I will be freed, no more illusions,
At last, I'll see your lovely face,
Dressed in a gown, bejeweled in sequins,
And feel again, your warm embrace.

When I lost you, life lost it's splendor,
I'll stay committed to His plan,
When from the balcony you wave,
We will renew, where we began.

October 30, 2018

Things Left Behind

I'm clearing drawers, and closets,
Giving her things away,
Recalling, her wearing clothes and garments,
And things, I gave away today.

My action brings a memory,
Each item has a past,
Her fashions, and apparel leaving,
The sentiment will always last.

I can see her smiling now,
As she directs me from above,
Helping proper distribution,
With her choices, passed on with love.

The elegance of her eye for style,
Will provide, and beautify, someone new,
An expression of her love and kindness,
She left behind for me to do.

If she were here, she'd match each selection,
With cosmetics, for a fresh new glow,
Then a scarf, purse, and some earrings,
Her refined magic, combining pieces that flow.

Things left behind are no longer needed,
She's now robed, in a gown far above,
Hoping things passed on, will be useful,
And worn, with her humble love.

November 4, 2018

Eternal Vows

Today, the snow is softly falling,
Like on the day you slipped away,
Summer flowers have all withered,
They will again, return in May.

Unlike our love that keeps on blooming,
Unconcerned with weather change,
Vows prearranged, for the next life,
No need, for a new exchange.

We were joined by a solemn vow,
Until death do us part,
A worthy vow, meant for both worlds,
Death can't separate, true loving hearts.

In Heaven, love blooms forever,
Flowers, won't have to wait for May,
Snow will not be softly falling,
And, you will never slip away.

November 9, 2018

Please Don't Wake Me

Please don't wake me, I may be dreaming,
It's a peaceful time for me,
I maybe, cruising down memory lane,
Or maybe, someplace I'd rather be.

I maybe forming words in rhyme,
Floating freely in the air,
In a tribute to my loved one lost,
And the lasting love we share.

I may be awake in a day dream,
And feel a friendly atmosphere,
When thoughts and memories meet in song,
My dream of her is crystal clear.

Please don't wake me, I may be praying,
Searching for His plan for me,
I maybe in the midst of angels,
In a dream, of where someday I'll be.

Please don't wake me,
I may be on my final journey,
When my life's beyond repair,
Please don't wake, or try to keep me,
I'll awaken, with my loved one waiting there.

November 11, 2018

He Has A Reason

The Good Lord always has a reason,
In time we learn to understand,
It maybe a message from an angel,
Or one sent ahead, to lend a hand.

Love is the beauty of His nature,
Compassion disposed by His command,
I know my disappointments have a purpose,
I trust His reason, I trust His plan.

When the one I love left this world,
I asked why Lord, why not me?
A reason with His compassion,
On bended knee, He heard my plea.

I've been left behind for a reason,
He has unfinished work for me,
While I struggle for an answer,
He will guide until I see.

The Good Lord joined us for a reason,
I was blessed, the day she took my hand,
Our promised bond will last eternal,
I'm thankful, I await completion of His plan.

November 16, 2018

Please Be Waiting

Will you be there, waiting for me,
Like you were when I'd come home,
Don't be mad if I'm a little late,
Cause the Boss Man gave me overtime,
Sorry, I don't mean to have you wait.

He found things I haven't finished,
You know me, I procrastinate,
I have old work left to finish,
And some new work still to do,
That's why I'm running late.

I don't know when I'll finish,
So far He didn't say,
When my job is done,
He will let me know,
And send me on my way.

There maybe things still hidden,
He will teach from day to day,
I will learn, and pay attention,
Again, till now He didn't say.

I hate to keep you waiting,
You understand, it's not for me to say,
When the Boss Man says my job is done,
Please be waiting, I'll hurry on my way.

November 18, 2018

Adrianne My Queen

She made me feel like a king.

If you were to trace my DNA,
You'd find no royal blood in me,
But when she held me close,
And loved me, I felt like royalty.

A king without a kingdom,
A queen without a throne,
A simple life without a palace,
We just shared a loving home.

A queen, who deserved a Crown,
Her bloodline wasn't royal,
But, there was royalty about her,
And her heart was true and loyal.

With attributes more than suitable,
For a new domain, with His Majesty,
If you spent time in her presence,
I know you wouldn't disagree.

Her palatial home is now in Heaven,
Where my queen deserves to be,
With the real King and His Kingdom,
And His prevailing royalty.

November 20, 2018

Thanksgiving Dream

You were standing alone
with a hello smile,
Then you slowly came to me,
I held you, and we talked awhile,
Oh, what a sight for me to see,
But it was only a dream.

You still looked the same, nothing changed,
Your familiar glamor passing through,
Just like the many pictures,
I've framed and stored of you,
But it was only a dream.

A dream that lasted longer,
Than other dreams before,
I treasure every dream of you,
I will always welcome more.

It was only a dream, but special,
It arrived Thanksgiving Day,
Thank you for your visit, I love you,
Together we'll celebrate someday,

When my dream of you comes true.

Thanksgiving Day
November 22, 2018

Her Heart Beat

Sometimes, when I close my eyes,
I feel our hearts in rhyme together,
A special transmission from Heaven,
In perfect rhythm lasting forever.

Amplified, across the bosoms of two souls,
Who for now are far apart,
Providing a pulse of soothing comfort,
Until my earthly heart, and soul depart.

I wait beneath, in this lower place,
Where her heart beat still resounds,
Pervading the space, time will erase,
When we meet again, on solemn ground.

Her precious heart was true and giving,
I'm not surprised it lingers on,
Her heart, was always there when needed,
A foundation I still depend upon.

A message without words or waver,
An expression served from above,
So, I'll close my eyes and listen,
For her heart beat, laced with love.

November 27, 2018

You Didn't Mean To Break My Heart

On a cold winter morning
You left me here alone.
My world stood still, then fell apart.
Your departure premiered in Heaven.
You didn't mean to break my heart.

My loneliness came in exchange,
For your warm, eternal start.
A willing trade, with love I made.
You didn't mean to break my heart.

It took some time to understand.
He has a reason, we're set apart.
His plan for you, was for me too.
You didn't mean to break my heart.

You didn't mean to break my heart.
I trust His plan for me and you.
I'll carry on while He directs me.
His love like ours is tried and true.

My broken heart someday He'll mend,
When His plan for us comes to an end,
I'll be with you once again,
And, I know Sweetheart,
You didn't mean to break my heart.

December 1, 2018

Special Days

You were held in Heaven
For Easter on your birthday.
I saved your valentine for Mother's Day.
Halloween had children at our door,
With pumpkins, and your scarecrow on display.

Your Thanksgiving wreath was on the door,
Our boys called, with thankful greetings.
Your chair was empty at the table.
It was hard to share Thanksgiving feelings.

Christmas will be another marker.
Then, New Year's Eve with little cheer,
Without you, special days aren't easy.
Missing you, and memories bring a tear.

Special days will duplicate next year,
With only your spirit passing through.
For now, the only joy is knowing,
Someday, I'll celebrate,
Special days with you.

December 4, 2018

When Tomorrow Is Forever

When tomorrow is forever,
You will lead me by the hand.
To meet our Mothers and the others,
Who paved the way to Glory Land.

I'll see their smiles and hear their laughter,
I've been missing for some time.
When tomorrow is forever,
A new beginning with endless time.

Only joy, no more sorrow,
Joining friends and family cloaked in white.
When tomorrow is forever,
And yesterday is out of sight.

With angels above us soaring,
Gray skies will now be blue.
When I inherit tomorrow,
I'll spend forever with you.

December 10, 2018

Framed and Saved

You're surrounded by angels in Heaven,
While frames surround pictures at home.
Pictures framed and surrounded with memories,
A reminder of times we have known.

The picture of you I most treasure,
Has a place in front of my mind.
It's always with me, whenever I go,
And can never be left behind.

A picture captured one evening,
Stored by the lens in my mind.
You reached for me from your bedside,
Saying, "come here, I love you," one last time.

A moment framed and developed from Heaven,
I'll remember the smile on your face,
And your words spoken so clearly,
When we shared a final embrace.

I know angels were present,
Like those who surround you above.
A gift framed and saved from our Saviour.
An expression of lasting true love.

December 12, 2018

Every Now And Then

Every now and then,
I lose track of time.
I can't remember when it was,
You were not somewhere in my mind.

I know it wasn't yesterday,
Or the day before, and I'm
Sure it wasn't last year,
Or anytime the year before.

Every now and then,
I send my memory back in time,
And there may have been
A day or two when thoughts of you
Were missing from my mind.

Since you left our home for Heaven,
I have no memory loss of time,
No longer every now and then, but always,
Thoughts of you never leave my mind.

When thoughts of you turn into dreams,
And I see us together again.
Such thoughts and dreams bring comfort,
Every now and then.

December 16, 2018

Adrianne's Mother Mary

There are many angels in heaven,
Adrianne's Mother Mary is one,
I often heard their discussions,
As if she were here one-on-one.

Although the exchange was one-sided,
An appeal was never denied,
At least when the session was over,
She always appeared satisfied.

Sometimes it was nighttime chatter,
Or a plea because of confusion,
She always knew who to turn to,
I know this was not a delusion.

Whenever she called out for Mama,
I'm sure she was soon by her side,
Dually assigned, both angelic and Mother,
For a daughter,
She once mothered with pride.

They are now paired together forever,
Though Mary's works far from done,
She has children yet to call on,
And prove my story isn't homespun.

2018

Adrianne's Special Heart

Her spirit was always uplifted,
When she watched the Shriner's ad,
Alec, the boy in a wheelchair,
Caused attention to the love she had.

I often observed her devotion,
When children appeared on the screen,
Her eyes would light up undivided,
God blessed her with that special gene.

In spite of the challenge she faced,
Her heart was never disabled,
As daughter, sister, aunt, spouse, and mother,
She gave all the love she cradled.

Her laughter and gentle good nature,
Never found room for a strife,
What a wonderful resource for heaven,
Her example for eternal life.

She's now surrounded with children,
Their names, she reclaims everyone,
Restored with total redemption,
Her reward for a job well done.

2018

Please Help Thy Neighbor

Today, I saw a couple,
While at my daily haunt,
I didn't ask, but I could tell,
A familiar need and want.

I know too well the story,
I witnessed on this day,
Her obvious confusion,
Was fully on display.

He gently helped her to their car,
And, as they drove away,
A sadness then came over me,
And I took some time to pray.

I know what he is going through,
And facing every day,
With little hope of any change,
That time might send their way.

My heart goes out to you my friend,
Just bravely bear your cross,
Provide the help within your means,
I understand the cost.

2018

False Appearance

Don't be fooled by false appearance,
No one can see my heart,
It's torn in many pieces,
And it's tearing me apart.

I'm searching for a treatment,
I'm not sure one can be found,
To mend tormented fragments,
Of a love so tightly bound.

When, in advance you know the outcome,
And what the final's going to be,
You're not prepared, for days that follow,
The looming pain you can't foresee.

If I had a window in my heart,
My true appearance you would find,
Lacking noticeable improvement,
For this damaged heart of mine.

Father Time may have some answer,
Giving darkened days some light,
Still my heart and my appearance,
Will never be alike.

Mother's Day 2018

Footprints in the Snow

Footprints at her graveside,
In the freshly fallen snow,
One may wonder why I visit,
When her soul has found a region,
Far above and not below.

This question I still ponder,
For it's here I said goodbye,
Or it may be one more "Here I am,"
With the hope, she might reply.

I sense that she can see me,
I know her watchful eye,
While seated by a fountain,
From her vantage point on high.

When I stop by to say hello,
It may provide a chance,
She might reminisce the moment,
And remember our last dance.

She may come on angel wings,
Or beam from her shining star,
Recognize, I stand here praying,
Then, to me softly whisper, "There you are."

2018

Happy Mother's Day, Mom

I won your heart,
And you won mine,
Then our boy's won a Mother,
Who was one of a kind.

Today they count their blessings,
Thank a Mom who was so true,
Through tearful eyes they send their love,
This Mother's Day to you.

They know how much you love them,
Your heart always made that clear,
This year's absence makes no difference,
In their hearts you're always here.

You nursed them from the cradle,
Supported growth from day to day,
Encouraged them when they had doubts,
In your loyal and loving way.

Today, they're nourished by the memory,
Of love you freely gave away,
They know again, you've made room for them,
To celebrate, someday together,
On a future Mother's Day.

Mother's Day 2018

Here I Am

Waiting for your spirit,
To pass by my lonely door,
Praying you'll decide,
And spare the time,
To share a glimpse once more.

You may come, well disguised,
In a brilliant glistening light,
Or a puff of milky blue,
No matter how you come to me,
My dear, I'll know it's you.

As you glide by, without a word,
I'll throw a kiss your way,
And watch you vanish like a dream,
With no intent to stay.

I'll forever keep an eye out,
In case I'm in your plan,
I still recall, when you would say,
"There you are!"
And once again my love,
"Here I am!"

As for now I'll hope and pray,
You'll forgive my heart's refrain,
And redecorate a moment,
Please pass my way again.

2018

It Will Never Be the Same

Days are long and dreary now,
My nights are filled with pain,
I toss and turn from dusk till dawn,
It will never be the same.

No one to say "good morning" to,
Or greet to start the day,
He left this world, and me alone,
When his soul was swept away.

Empty days are dull and lonely,
His absence, can't be reclaimed,
One thing I know, without a doubt,
It will never be the same.

I daydream now of days gone by,
Of times I held him near,
I'm flooded with his memories,
One by one they reappear.

Holding on to all the reasons why,
What our true love became,
Will have to offer comfort now,
But it will never be the same.

2018

Lost and Found

Whenever something's missing,
That's normally around.
It might be human nature,
To check the lost and found.

But when you have a loved one,
Pass peacefully alone,
You can trust, they will be found.
Found in the arms of Jesus,
With choirs of angels all around.

The home my true love left one morning,
Served a purpose in the past,
The first part of her journey,
She found her final home at last.

So if you have someone missing,
That's normally around,
Thank the sacrifice of Jesus,
Who provides a lost and found.

Thank you, Jesus

2018

Reflection

For those of you
Who have yet to face a time,
When called to give your all,
Embrace the gift your given,
It's time to stand up tall.

Give repentance for times you failed,
Or overlooked a need,
Preferring your poor choices,
When your loved one disagreed.

It's time to make repayment,
For all the love she gave,
Ignoring all the failures,
And disappointments she forgave.

Regardless of the challenge,
The Lord will guide the way,
I know from whence I speak,
Your solemn vows you can't betray.

When it's time to seize the moment,
Make sure that you are there,
To help the one who loves you,
When hopeless with despair.

Though, assistance and contrition,
Alone will not restore,
She'll leave this world knowing,
You regret, you weren't able to do more.

2018

Teardrops on My Pillow for a While

I left my home this morning,
To face another day,
An empty house behind me,
And, no goodbyes to say.

When I return this evening,
There will be no friendly smile,
No one to hold and care for,
Only teardrops on my pillow for a while.

Some say, "Find a new companion,
to ease your days of gloom."
But, my broken heart's not vacant,
There is no need or any room.

I fill my thoughts with better days,
Good times, too many, to compile,
Then sorrow overwhelms my mind,
More, teardrops on my pillow for a while.

We vowed, life and death together,
When we walked that sacred aisle,
A consecrated oath forever,
There'll be "teardrops on my
pillow for a while."

2018

The Blood of Jesus

I know where I am going,
He said, a room is saved for me,
And promised I will find you there,
When He decides to set me free.

So this lonely road I travel,
Is filled with thoughts of you each night,
I wait to see, your precious smile again,
Until He says my time is right.

This painful separation,
A willing price I'm called to pay,
In return for your eternal rest,
Restored in comfort every day.

I still have some work to finish,
His plan for me I can't foresee,
I will trust our Savior's promise,
Again, united we will be.

I will find you in His garden,
I'll no longer be alone,
We will celebrate together,
When the blood of Jesus leads me home.

St. Patrick's Day 2018

There You Are

I tucked her in our bed each night,
With a kiss, then slowly slipped away,
Though I never wandered far.
On my return, with a smile she'd say,
"There you are!"

Together we would say a prayer,
And wish each other well.
I miss that special moment now,
Much more than words can tell.

When my remaining days elapse,
I'll pursue her shining star,
And find my way,
To hear her say, once more,
"There you are!"

2018

Her New Life

This winding road we travel,
With all the turns and bends,
And sometimes hills and valleys,
Leaves us wondering where it ends.

Our lives will not end here my friend,
There are brighter days ahead,
Where gardens grow and fountains flow,
And our lost loved ones proudly tread.

They can't come back to tell us,
Of the splendor they enjoy,
Or their view of soaring angels,
Our Savior chooses to deploy.

How earthly pains and problems,
Like soiled clothes are shed,
Now more alive than ever,
New life fulfilled instead.

My loved one walks among them,
I'm sure wishing I could see,
How beautiful her new life is,
And planning to make room for me.

2018

Could've, Should've, but Didn't

You deserved a better life than I provided,
My regretful heart's forever weighted,
Through trials and failings, you never complained,
When good ambitions were not completed.

I could've, should've, but didn't,
I should've known, God's in charge, not me,
I could've listened and considered, but didn't,
And many efforts failed to be.

Too often success, too soon proclaimed,
My controlling nature foiled again,
I should've seen the ending, but didn't,
Once again you could've, but never complained.

Always beside me, you could've left, but didn't,
I was never surprised, for that was you,
Whenever discouraged, you always encouraged,
From beginning to end, our whole lives through.

I should've made life better, but didn't
So the One in charge said,
"Son, you could've, but you didn't,
I know you tried,
Don't look back, just step aside,
And I'll provide, a better life in heaven."

Happy fifty-second anniversary, hon.
Love, Charles.

A Path Prepared

He prepared a path for me to follow,
I trust it leads me right to you,
There may be valleys on my journey,
And, I might miss a step or two.

He will lift me should I stumble,
And extend His helping hand,
With inspiration, I will move along,
Giving heed to His commands.

On days when I'm disheartened,
And, slip from His gracious hand,
He reminds me, don't look down,
Keep looking up, He has a perfect plan.

Looking down will cause a falter,
It will blur His guided way,
I'll look up and pay attention,
As He leads me night and day.

His promised pathway is well traveled,
I know it leads me back to you,
I'll stay on the path He has provided,
I won't waiver, I'll follow through.

Not to trust His promise, I'd be remiss,
Who could doubt a path and plan like His?

Charles Buzzell
February 22, 2019

Note

"Adrianne"
Our hearts were joined by God,
back in the sixties.
Our love engraved right from the start,
And when I make my way to heaven,
He'll find your name, Adrianne,
Still branded on my heart.

About the Author

C harles Buzzell grew up in Anoka County and is the eldest of twelve children. He was raised by a mother and a father who instilled a love of God in his life. As he grew, he always remembered to let God be his guide. In August of 1966, he met and married his beautiful wife, Adrianne, and together they raised two boys. Charles and Adrianne lived and loved one another for nearly fifty-two years. In 2009, Charles's wife was diagnosed with Alzheimer's disease, and life as they knew it changed. Throughout their journey, Charles devoted himself to caring for his beautiful wife and worked fervently to ensure her quality of life. In January of 2018, his wife, Adrianne, earned her angel wings. Today, Charles is seventy-nine years old, is self-employed, and is semiretired. From the loss of his wife and experience with this disease, he has been moved to write this tribute. Charles's prayer is that all who read his prose will be reminded of God's promise of eternal life, rest, and restoration. Finally, while Charles is an untrained author, you will soon see how God has spread His message of hope through him to bless others on their journey of recovery.

CPSIA information can be obtained
at www.ICGtesting.com
Printed in the USA
BVHW031908201119
564396BV00001B/100/P

9 781644 244654